Sign Language & Animals

Bela Davis

Abdo Kids Junior
is an Imprint of Abdo Kids
abdobooks.com

abdobooks.com

Published by Abdo Kids, a division of ABDO, P.O. Box 398166, Minneapolis, Minnesota 55439.
Copyright © 2023 by Abdo Consulting Group, Inc. International copyrights reserved in all countries.
No part of this book may be reproduced in any form without written permission from the publisher.
Abdo Kids Junior™ is a trademark and logo of Abdo Kids.

Printed in the United States of America, North Mankato, Minnesota.

102022

012023

THIS BOOK CONTAINS
RECYCLED MATERIALS

Photo Credits: Shutterstock

Production Contributors: Teddy Borth, Jennie Forsberg, Grace Hansen

Design Contributors: Candice Keimig, Pakou Moua

Library of Congress Control Number: 2022937161
Publisher's Cataloging-in-Publication Data

Names: Davis, Bela, author.

Title: Sign language & animals / by Bela Davis

Description: Minneapolis, Minnesota : Abdo Kids, 2023 | Series: Everyday sign language | Includes online
        resources and index.

Identifiers: ISBN 9781098264055 (lib. bdg.) | ISBN 9781098264611 (ebook) | ISBN 9781098264895
        (Read-to-Me ebook)

Subjects: LCSH: American Sign Language--Juvenile literature. | Animals--Juvenile literature. | Deaf--
        Means of communication--Juvenile literature. | Language acquisition--Juvenile literature.

Classification: DDC 419--dc23

Table of Contents

Signs and Animals

ASL is a visual language. There is a sign for all your favorite animals!

ANIMAL

1. Touch and hold the fingertips to the chest while keeping the fingers straight

2. Move hands toward each other twice without the fingers leaving their place

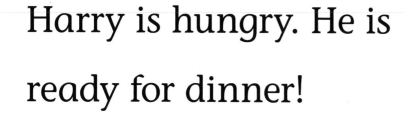

Harry is hungry. He is
ready for dinner!

CAT

1. Make the "F" sign but separate the thumb and index finger by an inch
2. Place the hand near the bottom of the nose and move it away while closing the thumb and index finger

Baily has her favorite chew toy.

She is ready to play!

DOG

A. Sign "D" then snap the thumb and middle finger as you quickly change to "G"

B. Or you can simply pat your leg twice with an open hand

The bunny is white
and fluffy.

BUNNY/RABBIT

1. Make the "U" sign with both hands

2. Cross the wrists, placing one on top of the other

3. Wiggle the middle and index fingers back and forth a couple times, like bunny ears

The bird is colorful!

BIRD

1. Make the "G" sign
2. Place the hand up by the mouth
3. Open and close the thumb and index finger twice

13

The monkey is curious.

MONKEY

1. Bend both elbows with hands down near the waist
2. Fingers should be a bit curled like a monkey's
3. Pull the hands up toward the armpits twice

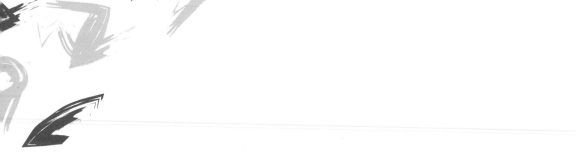

The tiger cleans itself
with its tongue.

TIGER

1. Bring both open hands up to the face, palms facing in and fingertips on either side of the nose

2. Pull hands apart at the same time

The horse runs quickly
through the field.

HORSE

1. With one hand, extend the thumb, index, and middle fingers into an L shape
2. Touch the thumb to the temple with the index and middle fingers pointed upward
3. Move the index and middle fingers up and down at the same time

The shark swims slowly in the ocean.

SHARK

1. Hold one hand, palm flat, straight up in front of you (this is the shark's fin)
2. With the other hand, split the fingers between the middle and ring finger
3. Place the shark fin between those two fingers
4. Keep the hands connected and move them forward and side-to-side, in a swimming motion

The ASL Alphabet!

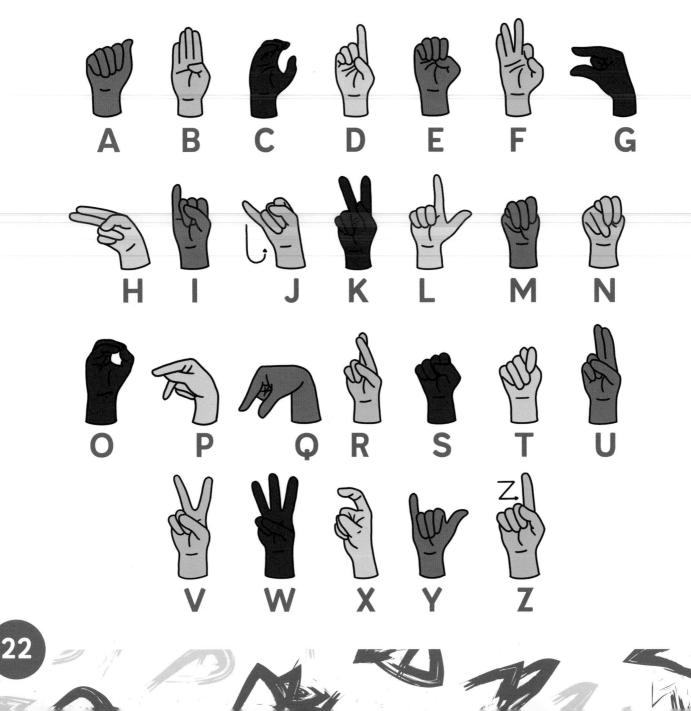

Glossary

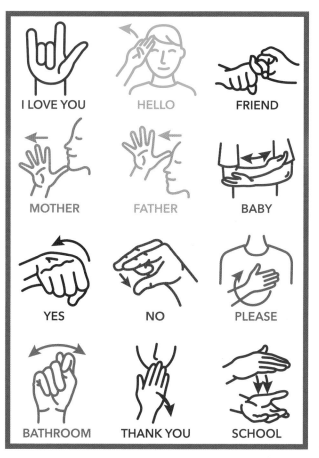

ASL

short for American Sign Language, a language used by many deaf people in North America.

curious

eager to learn or know.

Index

Abdo Kids
ONLINE
FREE! ONLINE MULTIMEDIA RESOURCES

Visit **abdokids.com**
to access crafts, games,
videos, and more!

Use Abdo Kids code
ESK4055
or scan this QR code!